MARIANNE JEWELL MEMORIAL LIBRARY
BAKER COLLEGE OF MUSKEGON
MUSKEGON, MICHIGAN 49442

PASSPORT SOUTH AFRICA

D1408021

Passport To The World

Passport Argentina
Passport Brazil
Passport China
Passport France
Passport Germany
Passport Hong Kong
Passport India
Passport Indonesia
Passport Israel
Passport Italy
Passport Japan
Passport Korea
Passport Malaysia
Passport Mexico
Passport Philippines
Passport Poland
Passport Russia
Passport Singapore
Passport Spain
Passport Taiwan
Passport Thailand
Passport United Kingdom
Passport USA
Passport Vietnam

PASSPORT
SOUTH
AFRICA

Your Pocket Guide
to South African
Business, Customs & Etiquette

Charles Mitchell

Passport Series Editor: Barbara Szerlip

WORLD TRADE PRESS®
Professional Books for International Trade

MARIANNE JEWELL MEMORIAL LIBRARY
BAKER COLLEGE OF MUSKEGON
MUSKEGON, MICHIGAN 49442

World Trade Press
1505 Fifth Avenue
San Rafael, California 94901 USA
Tel: (415) 454-9934
Fax: (415) 453-7980
E-mail: WorldPress@aol.com
http://www.worldtradepress.com

"Passport to the World" concept: Edward G. Hinkelman
Cover design: Peter Jones/ Marge Wilhite
Illustrations: Tom Watson

Passport South Africa
Copyright © 1998 by World Trade Press. All Rights Reserved.

Reproduction of any part of this work beyond that permitted by
the United States Copyright Act without the express written per-
mission of the copyright holder is unlawful. Requests for permis-
sion or further information should be addressed to World Trade
Press at the address above.

This publication is designed to provide general information con-
cerning the cultural aspects of doing business with people from a
particular country. It is sold with the understanding that the pub-
lisher is not engaged in rendering legal or any other professional
services. If legal advice or other expert assistance is required, the
services of a competent professional person should be sought.

Library of Congress Cataloging-in-Publication Data
Mitchell, Charles, 1953-
Passport South Africa: your pocket guide to South African business, customs & etiquette / Charles Mitchell.
p. cm. -- (Passport to the world)
Includes bibliographic references.
ISBN 1-885073-19-4
1. Corporate culture -- South Africa. 2. Business etiquette -- South
Africa. 3. Negotiation in business -- South Africa. 4. Intercultural
communication. I. Title. II. Series.
HD58. 7. M566 1997
390'. 00968--dc21
97-25259 CIP

Printed in the United States of America

Table of Contents

South Africa

The Continent's Savior?

South Africa
Quick Look

Official name   Republic of South Africa
Land area   470,462 sq mi (1.2 million
                        sq km)
Largest city   Johannesburg (pop. 1.9
                        million)
Capitals
  Administrative   Pretoria
  Legislative   Cape Town
  Judicial   Bloemfontein
People
  Population   44 million
  Annual growth   2.7%
  Language   Eleven official ones, with
                        English, Afrikaans, and
                        Zulu the most popular
  Religion   Christian, Islam and
                        Hinduism
Economy
  GDP   US$118.6 billion
  Per capita   US$3,081
  Foreign trade
    Imports   US$26.6 billion
    Exports   US$27.3 billion
    Surplus   US$0.7 billion
  Trade partners   U.K., Germany
  Currency   1 Rand (R) = 100 cents
  Exch. rate (6/97)   R4.47 = US$1
Education and Health
  Universities   17
  Physicians   1 per 1,271 persons
  Life expectancy   Women – 65 years
                        Men – 59 years
  Infant mortality   66 per 1,000 live births

SOUTH AFRICA

Country Facts

Geography & Demographics

South Africa, as it's name implies, lies at the southern tip of the continent of Africa, the great wedge that divides the Atlantic and Indian Oceans. Its land mass is about twice the size of the American state of Texas, and there are few major inland rivers or lakes. Rich in gold (approximately 50% of total world production), diamonds, copper, coal and platinum, the only major mineral deposits not found here are petroleum and bauxite. Agricultural products (about 6% of the GDP) include citrus fruit, corn, dairy products, sugarcane, tobacco, wine and wool, and the country is the world's largest supplier of mohair (from Angora goats).

South Africa is also blessed with a diversity of dramatic landscapes. Located to the east of the Cape region is the Drakensburg, a mountainous area that contains the bulk of the country's mineral deposits. Along the northwest border with Botswana is the Kalahari Desert. The Great Karoo, a semi-arid basin of scrub land and hills, lies between the Cape and Drakensburg's mountain ranges.

Much of the interior consists of a high, semi-arid plateau known as the Veldt.

Until 1991, South African law divided the population into four major racial categories, Africans (Blacks), Whites, Colored and Asians, and interracial marriage was prohibited. Africans comprise about 75% of the population and are divided along ethnic or tribal lines into dozens of sub-groups. Whites (13.6% of the population) are primarily the descendants of Dutch, English, French and German settlers. Coloreds (8.6%) are descendants of early European settlers, slaves imported from the Dutch Indies and the indigenous people. The Asian or Indian community (2.6%) are the progeny of indentured servants brought here from India by the British colonial government in the mid-19th century to work on sugar plantations. It was only in 1961 that the notion to repatriate them was abandoned and they were allowed to remain as permanent residents. There's a small Chinese population, brought in to work on railroads and sugar estates. A small Portuguese community sprung up in the 1970s after fleeing independence wars in neighboring Angola and Mozambique (both former Portuguese colonies). Currently, about 57% of the population lives in urban areas; the number is growing because of the freedom of movement and residence recently allowed blacks and because of the high unemployment in rural areas.

Climate

Because of elevation changes and its coastal position, South Africa has a broad range of climates. The average daily number of sunshine hours are among the highest in the world. The southwest near Cape Town has a Mediterranean climate with dry summers and winter rainfall. (However, beware the

February-March winds. At their worst, they make "Windy City" Chicago's seem like light summer breezes.) Most of the rest of the country experiences summer rainfall, usually in the form of afternoon thundershowers. The Natal/KwaZulu coastal area has a humid subtropical climate, while the northern part of the country has a tropical climate. The interior (the Free State and southern Gauteng) have a temperate grassland-type climate (though it's been known to snow a couple of times a decade in Johannesburg), while desert and semi-desert conditions prevail in the Cape interior and the northwest. The mean annual temperature ranges from 23°C (73°F) in the north to 12°C (54°F) in the southern and eastern regions, with generally low humidity. The seasons are the reverse of the Northern Hemisphere's.

Several times a week, "miniquakes" shake Johannesburg. These tremors can be unnerving but aren't dangerous. They're caused by subterranean rock falls and adjustments in the gold mines (the deepest is the Crown Mines shaft that's more than three kilometers deep) around the city and aren't related to genuine earthquakes.

Business Hours

Generally, offices and shops are open Monday through Friday from 8 or 8:30 A.M. to 5 P.M., with 30 minutes to an hour for lunch. Toiling on the weekend is a no-no. Late-night shopping is rare, even in major urban areas. Banks and government offices generally operate between 9 A.M. and 3:30 P.M. Many banks and shops are open on Saturdays only until 11 A.M. Formerly, very strict "blue laws" forbade cinemas and shops to open on Sundays; even major sporting events were banned. Although these laws have been abolished, Sunday shopping remains a difficult task.

National Holidays:

New Year's Day . . . . January 1
Human Rights Day . . . . March 21
> Honors worldwide Human Rights movements and their
> role in dismantling apartheid.

Good Friday . . . . Varies
Family Day (a.k.a. Easter Monday). . . . . . Varies
Freedom Day . . . . April 27
> Anniversary of the country's first one-person-one-vote
> all-race election that brought Nelson Mandela to power
> and formally ended white-minority rule.

Worker's Day . . . . May 1
Youth Day . . . . June 16
> Commemorates those who died during the June 16,
> 1976 student uprising that protested mandatory school
> instruction in Afrikaans.

National Women's Day . . . . August 9
> Honors women who fought for the country's liberation.

Heritage Day. . . . . September 24
> Celebrates South Africa's diverse cultures and 11 official
> languages with regional festivals.

Day of Reconciliation . . . . .December 16
> (see "Changing Sensibilities" in Chapter 16)

Christmas Day . . . . .December 25
Day of Goodwill . . . . .December 26
> Known as Boxing Day in England, it has no particular
> relevance to South African culture.

When any holiday falls on a Sunday, the holiday is observed on the following Monday. Jewish holidays are observed on an individual basis with many companies permitting staff time off for religious purposes. Muslim holidays, including the fasting month of Ramadan, are also observed on an individual basis; the coastal regions have a relatively large Muslim population.

(For more on holidays, see Chapter 16: Customs.)

2 The South Africans

The White Tribe

In 1488, Bartholomeu Dias "discovered" the Cape, naming it "Cape of Storms," but his patron, King John of Portugal, foreseeing its potential as a trade route, decided on "Cape of Good Hope" instead. South Africa had been home to Hottentots, Zulus, Xhosas, Ndebeles, Vendas and other tribes for thousands of years (though little is known of their histories), and for the next 150 years or so, Europe left them alone.

When the Dutch first arrived in 1642, they did so as hired hands (rather than as colonists) on a mission to set up a provisions station for Dutch East Indies Company ships sailing around the continent's tip. Some thirty years later, they were joined by Germans and French Huguenots. Together, these groups became known as Afrikaners or Boers (Dutch for farmers).

Isolated and left to fend for themselves, the Boers soon lost all touch with Holland (and Germany and France) and became, in essence, another African tribe, albeit a white one. Increasing deviations from their original High Dutch, coupled with the need to communicate with various nationalities and local tribes, eventually created a separate language — Afrikaansche Taal or Afrikaans.

In 1814, the British gained possession of the Cape Colony and began abolishing slavery — which the Afrikaner/Boers believed was justified in the Old Testament and which, not coincidentally, made their farm economy possible. British rule also brought harsh discrimination against the Afrikaners in schools and employment. The migration that began in 1836, known as the Great Trek, inspired as many legends as the pioneer migration to the American West. Their possessions loaded into ox-drawn covered wagons, some 10,000 Afrikaners headed for the interior, doing battle along the way with the indigenous Ndebele and Zulu. Latter-day place names like Moordrift (Murder Ford) and Weenen (Weeping) recall their travails before establishing a series of republics in the Orange Free State and in Transvaal. But then, in 1886, diamonds and gold were discovered in Boer territory, and the resulting tensions escalated into the Anglo-Boer War (1899-1902), a conflict in which a young journalist named Winston Churchill won his first taste of fame. The Boers were defeated and in 1910, the self-governing Union of South Africa was established.

Apartheid

Although the post–World War II Afrikaner-dominated government of the Nationalist Party (which had been deeply sympathetic to Nazi Germany) generally gets the blame for introducing apartheid, racial segregation had its roots at least a generation earlier, during British colonial rule. The Natives' Land Act of 1912 expressly prohibited black Africans from owning land or sharecropping outside of designated reserves.

Still, it wasn't until the 1950s that the Nationalist Party government, under Henrdik Verwoed, began a concerted effort to codify into law its policy of "separate development of the races." The plan — meant to keep the white minority safe from what the Afrikaners called *Swart Gevaar* or Black Peril — was to purge the voting roster of all blacks and to create a system of residential "townships" or "homelands" (that is, ghettos) for all "non-whites" to live in. (Soweto, an abbreviation for South Western Township, became the most famous of these.) Some 3.5 million people were forced to relocate. The calculated result was 75 percent of the populace squeezed onto 15 percent of the land, most of it unfarmable.

A system of strict racial classification was introduced—one was either white, black, colored or Asian—and whether or not one was the latter often depended on the curl of one's hair. Interracial marriage, even interracial sex, was banned. "Non-whites" were required to carry identification (a.k.a. pass books) at all times. They flocked to the cities by day to work, but these same cities literally became white-by-night, as blacks and coloreds who wandered beyond their home areas after sundown risked being jailed or at least fined. Schools, too, were segregated, and the quality of black education was poor. The African National Congress (ANC), formed in 1912, came to prominence in the late 1950s as a protest movement. It was banned in 1960 and many of its leaders were jailed.

... And Its Demise

While both the U.S. and Western Europe condemned apartheid, they still counted South Africa as a staunch anticommunist Cold War ally. The collapse of the Soviet Union and end of the Cold War shifted the equation. In the 1980s, a multinationalist boycott of South African products and trade and a suspension from participation in the U.N. General Assembly exerted significant economic pressure. Internal pressure (from black labor unions, church groups, and enlightened corporations like the mining giant Anglo American) also contributed to apartheid's eventual collapse.

In 1989, Frederick Wilem de Klerk took office and began a series of reforms that included the desegregation of hospitals and other public facilities. In 1990, state schools were allowed to admit non-white pupils, and by 1994, they were forbidden to exclude them. De Klerk also freed anti-apartheid political prisoners, including ANC leader Nelson Mandela, who had languished in prison for 27 years. (De Klerk and Mandela were subsequently awarded the Nobel Peace Prize.) Three years later, in 1994, Mandela was elected South Africa's first black president by a 63 percent majority after the country's first "one-man one-vote" election, and the ANC became the ruling party.

Not only was apartheid (literally, apart-hood) a moral disaster, but it probably set back the country's economic progress by decades by excluding the bulk of the population from meaningful commerce and wealth-sharing. International economic sanctions, coupled with the shortsightedness of the white minority government, left a social, educational and wealth gap that will take years, and painful sacrifices by whites, to close. While the apartheid laws have now been taken off the books, the racial attitudes that enforced them still abound, especially in rural areas.

The Economic Engine

While South Africa accounts for just 4 percent of the surface area and 6 percent of the population of Africa, it accounts for 25 percent of the continent's gross domestic product, 40 percent of its industrial output, 45 percent of its mineral production, and 50 percent of its generated electricity.

It was the first country to successfully pioneer the process of extracting oil from coal; during the international oil embargo against South Africa, the process supplied up to 10 percent of the country's gasoline and oil needs. The country also developed (many believe with Israeli help) nuclear power generating capacity.

South Africa is both the richest country in Africa and the most inequitable in terms of wealth distribution. The richest 10 percent of the population (almost exclusively white) accounts for more than half of the nation's income, and the average monthly income of whites is more than two and half times that of blacks.

Language

Plunk yourself down in front of a TV or radio in South Africa and you'll eventually be exposed to most of the languages in common use — from the guttural utterances of Afrikaans, the distinctive tongue clicking (borrowed from Hottentot) of Xhosa, and the mellifluous flow and rhythm of Zulu to Greek, Portuguese and even Gujarati.

White South Africans are generally able to converse in both English and Afrikaans; many road and building signs are posted in both languages. Black South Africans, especially those with some elementary education, will speak their own native tongue and also have a working knowledge of Afrikaans and English.

"Kitchen Dutch," Zulu & Xhosa

While representing the very core of national identity for Afrikaners, Afrikaans is roundly derided as the language of the oppressor by blacks, as well as by many liberal, English-speaking whites. Its mandatory use in "township" schools for such basic courses as math and geography was the flashpoint that set off the 1976 Soweto riots — nationwide disturbances that proved to be a turning point in the country's political history.

To say that Afrikaners are paranoid about the future of their language, especially under black majority rule, is an understatement. Afrikaans, also referred to as Kitchen Dutch or Baby Dutch, has existed in written form for a little more than 100 years. Once one of only two official languages, it's now one of eleven. On the country's three state TV channels, Afrikaans gets less than 4 percent airtime, putting it on equal standing with Zulu and Xhosa. (English gets the lion's share.)

Zulu is the most important of the African languages, primarily because up to one-third of all South Africans can either speak or understand it. Though learning elementary Zulu has become a fad among foreign businesspeople, its potential as a medium to rival English or even Afrikaans is limited. The reasons are simple: The country's Zulu population is centered on the Indian Ocean's coastal region of Natal, and more importantly, the ANC is dominated by Xhosa speakers. (Mandela is from a Xhosa chief's family.)

English is the language of commerce; by and large, it's politically neutral. It's the language of choice among young black Africans who have an obsessive admiration for all things Western, especially when those things are American.

Race: Not Swept Under the Carpet

South Africans are remarkably frank about race. Because the issue is so out in the open, the country seems more able to deal with it than, say, the U.S. or Japan. The notion of "political correctness" in regard to racial matters has yet to arrive. It really is acceptable to talk about it and to ask questions, but avoid imposing any outside moralities.

Whites, especially Afrikaners, retain a parental-like attitude toward blacks, tending to view them as children in need of guidance. The flagrant racial epithets you might hear in an American ghetto or blue collar suburb are surprisingly absent. Although witnessing this attitude in action — for example, the scolding of a housemaid for breaking a dish — can be excruciating to a visitor, it's important to remember that it doesn't stem from evil intent.

How Blacks Feel About Whites

Now that the burden of apartheid has been lifted and the races can freely reside in the same neighborhoods, go to the same schools and work the same jobs, expectations run high within all socio-economic classes. But simply put, the greater the education level, the higher the expectations of getting a chunk of the potentially huge economic pie.

Such expectations are justified. The richest 10 percent of the population (until recently, almost exclusively white) still accounts for more than half of the nation's income. Yet poverty in South Africa has a black face. A total of 44 percent of the population — 16.3 million people in 2.7 million households — were below the official poverty line in 1993. A startling 95 percent of those households were black.

One would expect to find more intense bitterness and hatred toward whites, but to the credit of

Nelson Mandela's government, the focus hasn't been on punishment and retribution but rather on working toward sharing the wealth. Even before coming to power, the ANC dumped most of its Marxist rhetoric and its plans to nationalize private industry. It seems its Marxist orientation was more a ploy to secure money, arms and military training from the Soviet Union than it was a deep-seated belief in Communism.

By and large, blacks realize that they need white expertise — and wealth — and are thus grudgingly tolerant of the white presence. They'll work together, but don't expect them to be close friends.

Black Attitudes Toward Other Races

While there's respect for the wealth and power of whites, the same can't be said when it comes to black attitudes toward the country's other significant minorities — the coloreds and the Indians (see Chapter 1: Geography & Demographics). The relationship between blacks and coloreds has always been uneasy, partly because the coloreds enjoyed a higher status under apartheid.

The coloreds haven't supported the ANC as strongly as the ANC had hoped, and this has led to frustration and mutual distrust. In fact, the colored community sided with the old pro-apartheid National Party in preventing the ANC from gaining control of Western Province (the area that's home to Cape Town) during the 1994 national election. The coloreds believed that they would simply have been trading in a white master for a black one, and that they'd lose what limited privileges and advantages they had over blacks under apartheid.

The country's Indian/Asian population, while more absorbed into the black political mainstream than the colored's, is still resented as a more monied class that had greater privileges under apartheid and at times took advantage of black consumers — by overcharging them and underpaying black workers to build their retailing businesses.

A First-World Third-World Mix

If ever there was a country of contradictions, South Africa is it. Nowhere else in Africa, or perhaps in the world, is there such a mix of First World technology and economic structure and Third World poverty within such a small nation. South Africans themselves haven't yet figured out by whose standards they should judge themselves. By African standards, they're a superpower, but by First World benchmarks, they're still a developing nation. This has led to a national schizophrenia, of sorts.

Shaped by Calvinism

Sixty percent of the population are members of Christian congregations. Under Afrikaner rule, the country was extraordinarily conservative in its religious beliefs. The dominant Dutch Reformed Church, whose most extreme interpretation of the Bible equated blacks with the Devil, created a nation that not only feared God but also shut down on Sunday — no organized sports, no shopping, no movies. Today, the Dutch Reformed Church still plays a major role in the everyday life of most Afrikaners.

For fear of cultural contamination, the country didn't introduce television until 1976 (despite having the technological expertise), and then did so only after fierce debate in parliament. Nonetheless, TV was strictly controlled by government censorship (as was the news media under apartheid). Today, there are several independent radio stations.

In black communities, many Christians observe

African beliefs. During apartheid, black clergy served as a major voice of protest. Anglican Archbishop Desmond Tutu won the Nobel Peace Prize in 1984 for his leadership of the anti-apartheid movement and for his efforts to force reconciliation talks between whites and exiled black leaders.

In recent years, South African society has become more secularized. Sex shops and prostitution are alive, well and openly advertised (see Chapter 13), while church attendance has decreased. Still, visitors will score no points by being flip about religion here. The chances are that you're talking with someone who has high respect for such beliefs.

The Family

Within the black community, the extended family has traditionally played an important part in social and economic life. (White society, with its strong Christian tradition, is built around the nuclear family.)

But apartheid drove a wedge into black family unity that isn't easily or quickly remedied. A mother might work as a live-in domestic in a white area while her children remain at home in a segregated township, being taken care by other family members. Often, the male head of the household was in a similar position, working in a gold mine as a migrant laborer, living in a dormitory, and traveling home to see his family a few times a year. Today, the ramifications of this splintering are still being felt, especially in urban areas.

How South Africans See Themselves

All South Africans profess a passionate love of their land, but the legacy of three decades of apartheid has made everyone deeply aware of their country's racial and ethnic divides. You're not just a white South African, you're English or Afrikaner. Nor will you find anyone describing himself as a black South African. Rather, he or she is, for example, a Xhosa or a Zulu. Tribalism is still very much alive, and such affiliations remain at the base of the country's patronage system in business, government and education. (While there's been some blurring of these cultural subsets in the urban environment in recent years, it will take generations to eliminate a mindset that's been evolving since the Dutch arrived more than 350 years ago.)

Centuries-old feuds, especially between the Zulu and the Xhosa, still flare into violence on a regular basis. When the Afrikaners ruled, they employed a divide-and-conquer strategy that took advantage of these rivalries, sending in gangs of armed Zulu police to quell disturbances in other tribal areas. The wounds are still festering and remain the country's largest source of racial/ethnic tension. Still, since Mandela, South Africa seems to have a much more forward-looking approach than most other African nations, who still blame colonialism for many of their ills.

South Africans see themselves as victims (though some would say whiners). The whites are being victimized by the blacks, who are getting back what had been forcibly taken from them. The English-speaking minority were victimized by the Afrikaners, the Afrikaners were victimized first by the English and then by a morally self-righteous and misguided international community. The Zulus are being victimized by the Xhosas, who dominate the ANC. But this is all interfamily squabbling. When pitted against other nations of Africa, all South Africans assume an air of superiority and arrogance, firm in the belief that their nation has no rival.

Business and government leadership, both black and white, talk openly of being the dominate power, not just here but throughout the continent. To be mentioned in the same breath as such other potential (and often failed) African powerhouses as Nigeria is almost an insult. They prefer to be compared with Europe or the U.S. They see themselves as the saviors of Africa, morally wiser than the rest, and better educated, too, with a superior legal system and infrastructure, and more sophisticated business practices. The ANC is determined to show that a black-ruled Africa nation can succeed, not just for South Africans but for all African blacks.

Pride in Achievement

Entertainers, writers, athletes and medical pioneers here seem to transcend the color barrier, evoking pride in the majority of their countrymen. Perhaps South Africa's most famous entertainer is Miriam Makeba, a.k.a. "Mama Africa." (Makeba's ex-husband Hugh Masekela had an international hit with his song "Grazing in the Grass" in the 1970s.)

Renowned writers include Nobel Prize-winning novelist Nadine Gordimer; Alan Paton, whose *Cry the Beloved Country* is one of the most famous books ever to emerge from South Africa; Doris Lessing; Andre Brink; Breytan Breytenback; Laurens van der Post; J. M. Coetzee; playwright Athol Fugard; and Zulu poet Mazisi Kunene.

Internationally acclaimed sports heroes include Gary Player and Ernie Els in golf, Cliff Drsydale in tennis, and Zola Budd in track. Christiian Barnard of Cape Town's Groote Schur Hospital put South African medicine on the map when he performed the world's first heart transplant in 1967.

3 Cultural Stereotypes

Racism

All whites are racists.

Whites are certainly race-conscious, as are blacks, and all hold strong views about other ethnic groups — not all of them flattering. As a general rule, the amount of prejudice white South Africans hold against blacks is in inverse proportion to their education level. But even high-level corporate executives will, claiming to be realists, dismiss blacks as incapable of meeting their standards. There's a strange, circular logic at work here. Whites will say they're not prejudiced but that blacks lack the education and experience needed to advance. But the very reason blacks were denied these opportunities under apartheid was because of their race.

As the country is exposed to more outside influences, white South Africans no longer automatically dismiss a foreigner of color as inferior or incapable of business expertise (especially if that person can help them make money). In rural areas, however, whites still view themselves as a cut or two above black Africans.

Afrikaners

The "hairy-backs" or "rock-spiders" are backward.

Historically, the Afrikaners have been closely associated with the land. The conventional wisdom is that they're simple with a less-than-sophisticated world view. While there's some truth to this, it's also true that Afrikaners successfully run some of the country's largest mining houses and banks.

The stereotype of "the dumb Afrikaner" is re-enforced through "the van der Merwe joke," the equivalent of the Irish or Polish joke elsewhere. Ol' Van, known for wearing knee-high socks with a pocket comb stuffed into one of them, is depicted as a bumbling, culturally challenged idiot. An example of such humor: Why did van der Merwe's chicken farm fail? Answer: He buried the chickens too deep.

Black Malice

Blacks hate whites because of apartheid and are just waiting to exact revenge.

The black Pan-Africanist Party, which campaigned in the 1994 general election on the slogan "One Settler, One Bullet" (settler meaning whites), failed to secure a substantial popular following and has since been almost totally discredited as the lunatic fringe. In fact, considering the impact of apartheid on the daily lives of Africans, the level of resentment toward whites within the black community is remarkable low.

During the 1970s and 1980s, there were rumors circulating that on a given signal, the black house staff working in white residences would murder their employers. The paranoia was heartfelt, but the massacres never took place. Needless to say, whites are breathing easier these days. Blacks don't want blood, they want economic power.

Expectations

Now that apartheid is dead, blacks expect to have big houses, BMWs, golf club memberships and house-maids, but they don't expect to work for them.

Expectations vary within each socioeconomic class. Blacks with a university education and business/technological skills have the same expectations as their white counterparts. Blacks living in poverty in formerly segregated townships and shanty towns have more realistic expectations about what majority rule can do for them than most whites believe — they want access to government-supplied homes, electrification of their neighborhoods, and better drinking water, jobs and education.

Macho Men

Regardless of their race, South African men are chauvinists and homophobes.

South Africans tend to view everything — from driving a car to business negotiations to playing tennis — as a personal challenge to their manhood. For male visitors, it's important to play the game; they'll be challenged to something sooner or later.

Dirty jokes loaded with sexual innuendo still draw hearty laughter. Flirting and skirt-chasing are obsessions second only to soccer, rugby and drinking. Women are considered second-class citizens. Show sensitivity toward homosexuality or disdain for drinking or sports and you risk being labeled a *wuss* (the equivalent of a sissy).

Virtually all white South African males have served in the military, many of them in cross-border wars in Angola and Namibia, and they're proud of their service. In fact, South Africa is home to Executive Outcomes, a group of former anti-apartheid militants who now make their professional exper-

tise (e.g., bomb defusement, disarming urban gue-
rillas) available to other legitimate governments for
a fee, a service they describe as "putting out the
world's fires." They eschew the word "mercenary"
and even have a promotional video.

Unworldly

*South Africans, both black and white, have been iso-
lated for so long that they don't understand how the rest
of the world works.*

On the contrary, South Africans have always
been highly sensitive to outside opinion and attitudes. Urban South Africans, in particular, absorb
foreign cultures and business practices like
sponges. While in exile, leaders of the now-ruling
ANC had contact with many of the world's elite
politicians and businesses and received high marks
for their sophistication. On the home front, global
business giants like Anglo American Corporation
and De Beers have brought a surprising high level
of sophistication to bear.

In an effort to encourage foreign investment,
the ANC eliminated the nonresident shareholders
tax and limits on repatriation of hard currency in
1995, and no tax is charged for the importation of
capital goods.

A Violent Society

*South Africans are contentious and always looking
for trouble.*

It's true that there's still a "frontier mentality"
in South Africa, even in the major cities, where
most whites possess at least one firearm. Much of
the country's violent nature stems from its history.
At one time or another, just about everybody
fought everybody else.

Since the demise of the pass laws (which restricted when and where blacks could travel), crime has emerged from the segregated townships. A decade ago, writes *The Economist*, "whites dressed up to go to the theatre or dine out in central Johannesburg [and] blacks stepped off the pavement for them." Today, the city is "crowded with hawkers of boiled sweets and witch medicine [and] white businessmen scurry home at the end of the day." Muggings, armed robbery, car thefts and rapes are rampant. Many whites won't drive at night, and homes are being encased by security gates and (sometimes electrified) fences.

A structural breakdown in the once-white-dominated police force (which, during apartheid, concentrated on suppressing political dissent rather than on fighting crime) has exacerbated the situation. And the corruption is internal as well as external. Policemen in one vehicle-theft unit have been formally charged with running a vehicle-theft ring, and more than 200 members of the police VIP-protection service are facing criminal charges that include murder.

However, the appointment, as of August 1997, of Meyer Kahn as chief executive of the national police force suggests that the government is prepared to tackle the situation aggressively. Kahn is the chairman of South African Breweries, one of the world's top ten brewers. Whites approve of the appointment because Kahn is a successful, no-nonsense businessman of Lithuanian stock, while blacks like him because his company employs black managers and sponsors the country's soccer league. Moreover, adds *The Economist*, "Mr. Kahn is wonderfully unlike South Africa's patrician, sometimes arrogant, white mine owners."

Regional Differences

For all the talk about a unified South Africa, the country's long history of conflict and its contrasts in topography and lifestyle — from desert dwellers to urban sophisticates to salt-of-the-earth farmers to laid-back coastal inhabitants, along with concentrations of ethnic populations — have created a witches' brew of rivalries. South Africa's nine provinces are, by and large, divided along ethnic lines, each with its own favored cuisine, its own pace of business, its own powerhouse sports teams, and its own view on how the country should be run.

White residents at the coast are said to be inflicted with "Natal fever" — a malaise characterized by procrastination and a tendency to prefer the beach to the office. Tourists from inland are referred to in Natal as *Kak Daars* (Afrikaans for "Look there"), an expression that wide-eyed coastal neophytes tend to mouth as they stroll along Durban's "anything goes" beachfront.

Gauteng: Center of the Universe

When it comes to business, Gauteng province rules, at least for now, with Johannesburg at its center. Formerly known as the Transvaal (or, in the vernacular, as PWV — the *Pretoria Witwatersrand Vereeniging* triangle), Gauteng comprises just 2 percent of the country's land mass but more than 43 percent of its GDP and almost 50 percent of its manufacturing. It also accounts for much of the country's poor international image, crime-wise.

Founded by Afrikaners in the mid-19th century, the Transvaal Republic was a harsh land, seemingly of little value, until gold was discovered there in 1886. There's little real reason for Johannesburg to be situated where it is. It's some distance from the gold mines that supplied its wealth and it's the largest city on the African continent not located on a major body of water. According to local legend, mine workers ran out of railway ties and rails, and while waiting for resupply, a major settlement sprung up that became too big to move.

More than any other South African province, Gauteng provides sharp contrasts between rich and poor. Johannesburg's northern suburbs, home to the Mink and Manure Set (wealthy and horsey types) coexist rather uncomfortably with the poor urban blacks who are drawn like magnets to Egoli — "the City of Gold," as Johannesburg is still called in rural areas. Nowadays, it's not uncommon to see a wealthy northern suburb "madam" dressed to the nines, wandering through one of Sandton City's glittering shopping malls among unemployed, scruffily clothed township residents who are looking to pass the time and panhandle a few *rand* for food.

The building that houses the Johannesburg Stock Exchange (the tenth largest in the world in terms of market capitalization and, until recently, an exclusively white bastion of wealth and power) glimmers against the sky amid market stalls and sidewalk shacks — a constant reminder of both the country's potential wealth and the increasing gulf between the haves and the have-nots.

Blacks now control approximately 9 percent of the Johannesburg Stock Exchange, up from zero in 1991. In 1995, the Exchange opened its membership to foreigners, who subsequently bought 41.5 billion *rand* — US$9.5 billion — worth of South African equities. Insider trading, however, is a problem.

The region remains the center of theater, music, art and money. Like New Yorkers or Parisians, successful Johannesburgers, both black and white, tend to view residents of lesser cities as "the great unwashed" — people confined to unimportant lives in unimportant businesses in unimportant backwaters.

Free State: The Iowa of South Africa

The Free State is the country's farm and bible belt, home to South Africa's judicial capital, the city of Bloemfontein. (Cape Town is the legislative capital, and Pretoria the administrative capital.) Though now ruled by a black government at the provincial level, the Free State is home to the majority of white resistance to black rule; it's here that white separatists continue to dream of a whites-only homeland.

Natal: Zulu Dawn

The lush vegetation, the sprawling (albeit shark-infested) beaches, and the crushing humidity of coastal Natal (so named by Portuguese explorer Vasco da Gama, who sighted it on Christmas Day, 1497) give this region its justified reputation for casualness. But in the new South Africa, Natal is a political "problem child." The Zulu tribe, long the rival of the neighboring Xhosas, dominates this province and strongly resents the central government. Primarily settled by English-speaking whites, it's always been independently minded — and a thorn in the side of the deposed Afrikaner government and a center of ethnic violence.

The city of Durban is a cross between Atlantic City in the U.S., with miles of towering (and somewhat shabby) beachfront hotels, and Mombassa in Kenya, an African tropical seaport with an "anything goes" attitude. Much of Natal's local governance emanates from the Royal House of the Zulu tribe. Don't be surprised to see blacks armed with clubs and spears wandering the streets. A Zulu without a weapon is roughly the cultural equivalent of a Wall Street stock broker without a cellular telephone.

Cape Town: Final Refuge

For many white South Africans, the Western Cape has become the final refuge, the only province still run by a mostly white government. Improving telecommunications and the relative absence of crime are drawing businesses from Johannesburg to Cape Town in droves. Once deemed a quaint backwater of surfers, dropouts and artists, Cape Town (a.k.a. the Mother City) is now more expensive than central Johannesburg. Though the surfers and artists are still here, the city has undergone a building boom, due partly to its surprisingly serious bid to host the summer Olympic Games early in the next century.

The end of apartheid and the lifting of international sanctions have inspired an explosion in the local wine-growing industry and the end to one of the most popular wine jokes (told by whites) in the country, which concluded with the punch line: *South Africa is known for its superior whites.* (In truth, the reds are better. Part of the joke is that the white community has disdain for Reds — as in Communists.)

The rugged mountains and stormy waters off the Cape of Good Hope have given birth to scores of seafaring legends. The ancient Arab seamen of Sinbad's day claimed that Table Mountain, which overlooks the city, was a giant magnet that drew ships to the rock. The disappearance of Portuguese explorer Bartholomeu Dias near the Cape in 1490 is the basis of the legend of the The Flying Dutchman, a ghost ship that roams the world's oceans. Some of the most credible sightings of the Flying Dutchman date back to World War II, when two German U-boat commanders, hunting merchant traffic off the Cape, reported seeing an old sailing ship plowing the high seas not far from where Dias is said to have perished in a shipwreck some five centuries earlier.

Mysticism aside, Capetonians have always been more racially tolerant than other South Africans. The culture of the colored (mixed-race) community, concentrated in the Western Cape, is felt in both the region's distinct patois and in its cuisine, which has a strong Malaysian bent.

Eastern Cape

This is the cradle of the country's "black consciousness movement." However, the East Cape's political importance has faded with the emergence of black rule and Nelson Mandela's government of national unity. The area around the city of Port Elizabeth, home to several large automotive plants, is known as "the Detroit of South Africa." Enough said.

Government & Business

Privatization & the Redistribution of Wealth

Considering that Communism and Socialism were anathema to the old white minority government, that government did a remarkable job of accumulating assets and controlling the economy. (However, ANC inherited an economy suffering from 20 years of double-digit inflation.) More than 50 percent of the country's fixed assets were in government hands, and most still are. As recently as 1990, the ANC was vowing to further nationalize industry, but it dumped its neo-Marxist philosophy for the pragmatism of the real world. Though it has pledged to "restructure" its asset holdings in the near future by offering them to foreign investors, the government is still having trouble saying the "p" word — privatization — with heartfelt sincerity.

The challenge facing the government is how to redistribute the wealth without discouraging whites, who are the true wealth creators. A good indicator of the new-found intention to let market forces determine outcomes was the 1993 abolition of mandated price controls for all goods and services, except for deposits on soft drink bottles.

"Black Economic Empowerment"

While the idea of black control of the economy isn't new in Africa, the Mandela government's approach is. It believes that encouraging black private investment and using the market to create black wealth will work far better than expropriation and nationalization — two policies that have left a trail of bankruptcy, corruption and gun shy international investors across the continent. Whether ordinary black citizens will become risk-taking, share-owning capitalists remains to be seen.

The ANC's new macroeconomic plan is decidedly pro–free market, calling for increased union flexibility, a lowering of remaining tariffs on imports, and an end to currency control regulations. But the government is caught between a rock and a hard place. It's beholding to the black unions for support yet has come to the realization that the relatively high union wages have proven a hindrance to luring overseas investment.

White Corporations See the Light

Sensing that cooperation beats expropriation or legislation any day, several of the country's major white-owned corporations are now helping to create black wealth through the private sector. Anglo American, the mining and manufacturing giant, has sold off a 48 percent stake in its Johnnies Industrial Corporation (manufacturing, media and retail) to a black-owned consortium at a huge discount. Others are following suit.

Cynics claim that "black empowerment" merely means large, white-owned conglomerates are trying to buy off black aspirations by creating a black elite who would serve as a buffer between continued white privilege and the aspirations of the black poor. There's some credence to this. (While per capita income among blacks grew 10 percent on average between 1985 and 1995, it was a small, well-educated middle class who benefited, while the vast majority remain an underclass.) Still, getting some of the nation's wealth into black hands will ward off future government action that could be even more painful financially. It's a wise and farsighted strategy, a matter of survival rather than benevolence.

Heroes Of the Day

Thabo Mbeki, Mandela's heir apparent and the architect of the country's macroeconomic plan, has emerged as the darling of both industry and the overseas investment community, having lured more than 160 foreign companies into the country in just two years. Discussing what he envisions for South Africa by the early 21st century with the *New York Times*, Mbeki listed a great lessening of segregation and poverty, higher literacy levels, and a jumpstart on the information superhighway. "We don't have a huge communications infrastructure ... to dig up," he explained.

Another new titan is Dr. Nthato Motlana, Mandela's physician. He controls New Africa Investments Ltd., which grew, in a few short years, from a storefront operation into a giant venture capital firm controlling US$1.9 billion in assets. He and his deputy, Cyril Ramaphosa, former secretary general of the ANC, are two of the most sought after black businessmen in the country, in demand as much for their abilities as for their political connections.

... And Some Critics

In 1994, the ANC campaigned with the promise of providing a million new homes (as well as creating jobs and lowering crime) within five years. Though they've fallen short, it's also true that millions of South Africans have been provided with electricity and clean water for the first time.

Playing Hardball

Foreign businesspeople should be prepared to deal with the reams of red tape that will be thrown at them both by the central government and by provincial authorities. The latter now have a much stronger say in what business gets done on their turf than in the past; don't underestimate the difficulties they can create.

In addition, South African companies are used to having the local playing field all to themselves and they jealously guard their territory. Several foreign companies who've attempted to set up shop here say that the biggest obstacles are some rather unethical practices from local competitors — from threatening suppliers to leaning on local government officials to create roadblocks to market entry.

6 The Work Environment

Security Over Advancement

Though South Africans love money, they see no virtue in "workaholism." In many ways, the national approach of balancing work, play and family is rather European. South Africans will work hard, but they're reluctant to put in overtime or to work weekends. Four- to six-week annual vacations are common. Labor laws make it difficult to fire a worker, and most who sign on with a corporation early in their career expect a job for life. As in America, however, lifetime corporate positions are becoming less and less likely.

Corporate Pyramids

"Cross ownership" is the watchphrase, with just four major corporations — Anglo American, Sanlam, Rembrandt and SA Mutual — controlling more than 70 percent of the market capitalization of the Johannesburg Stock Exchange. This approach can make it difficult for foreign competitors to enter the market.

Emerging black venture capital firms, which in the past had condemned cross ownership as an impediment to black entry into business, tend to copy their white counterparts when structuring their own companies.

Seniority Counts

Big business is elitist, and decisions are made at the top. Innovation from the lower ranks is rare. South Africans are big on "dues paying," working up slowly through the ranks and using school and family connections to advance. Rarely will you see someone under the age of 40 in a position of power in larger corporations. Entrepreneurial skills are highly valued, especially in the black community, where experience in big-time business circles was made virtually impossible by apartheid.

On average, executive pay is 23 times that of a manufacturing employee, putting the country on a par with the U.S. (24 times) but decidedly higher than Britain (19 times), Germany (11 times) and Japan (9 times).

Middle Management: Under the Gun

As blacks begin to move into the corporate world through government-supported affirmative action programs, white middle managers see themselves as being under siege. While virtually every business and corporation, regardless of size, has instituted a program of equal opportunity and affirmative action for blacks, the reception in mostly white middle management circles has been nothing short of icy. While handing over political power to the black majority cost whites little in terms of economic power, the movement of blacks into business is viewed as a threat to white livelihoods, resulting in an enormous amount of racial tension and angst. One study on affirmative action programs found that 71 percent of companies that have instituted such programs encountered serious resistance from white managers.

There's a remarkable lack of guilt on behalf of whites about the depravations of apartheid. A black executive in charge of affirmative action programs at a large U.S. computer company says the first question that's usually asked by white middle managers is, "Why do we have to have equal opportunity programs?" She says whites are in an absolute state of denial about apartheid. This is where the great divide comes in post-apartheid South Africa. An example of this attitude: Whites often half jokingly refer to the government's policy of providing housing, jobs and better education for South African blacks, a scheme formally known as the Rehabilitation and Development Program or RDP, as the Revenge of the Dark People.

With the great uneasiness about what lies ahead for white South Africans, especially those with technical skills, they're always keen to know their odds of "gapping it" to another country. The usual targets are Canada, Australia and the U.S. After enduring days of lectures about the great prospects in the new South Africa by senior officials at computer and mining companies, one visiting American financial journalist was asked privately, by no less than six different people of varying executive status, about their chances of success should they "gap it" to North America.

In the Factory, Unions Rule

South Africa has one of the strongest labor union movements in the world. During the apartheid years, labor unions, whose members are overwhelmingly black, were at the forefront of local anti-apartheid protests. With the transition to

majority rule, their power has become a problem
for the black government. Though productivity is
relatively low by world standards, wages are high
— a turnoff to international investors. Political mili-
tancy is still rampant. The number of manpower
days lost to strikes in 1994, Mandela's first year in
office, reached 4 million, and in 1995 the number
was still at a remarkably high 1.5 million. The government and private sector solution? Tap union
pensions and draw the unions in as corporate
investors, giving them a stake in profitability and
competitiveness. In this way, it's hoped that the
unions will become less militant and more willing
to work with management to generate profits.

Ubuntu: Finding the Middle Ground

Ubuntu is a Zulu word meaning "sensitivity
toward the human condition," the importance of
relations between people at all levels. It's an exten-
sion of the stakeholder concept, which it predates.
Ubuntu has become a management/academic buzz
word as the country begins a transition from being
overtly European to becoming a blend of European
and African orientations. The *ubuntu* approach
stresses that there should be a middle ground, a
balance between "bottom line" performance and
the welfare of employees, and that businesses have
a social responsibility not only to their employees
and stockholders but also to the country and society as a whole. It tries to recreate the corporation as
a family unit, with each member expected to pull
their own weight in exchange for fair reward and
individual respect.

7 Women in Business

An Uphill Battle

Women are conspicuously absent as hero figures in the country's history, mainly because much of that history is based on armed struggles, from the pioneering days of the Voortrekkers to the guerrillas wars of the anti-apartheid movement — all, the province of men.

Traditionally, women were, and continue to be, responsible for home and family and absent from the power structure. (An interesting exception are the Lobedu, who elect a female ruler based, in part, on her ability to make rain.) Most South African men are unwilling to participate in any domestic chores, be they cooking, shopping, cleaning or childcare. In rural areas, polygamy is common and female education often an afterthought.

Because of the country's British heritage, women have always had the vote, and under civil law, they can initiate divorce (except in rural areas governed by tribal law) and own property and credit cards. Still, it's only since 1995 that married women have been permitted to make charitable donations in their own names for tax purposes. Previously, all donations were regarded as having been made by the husband.

The term "businesswoman" is largely an oxymoron within both the black and the white communities. South Africa remains an "Old Boys' Network," and it lags far behind other industrialized nations when it comes to hiring women for senior management positions. As the notion of black economic empowerment takes hold, it's black *men* who are assuming the influential roles.

It's not uncommon for women employees to be referred to as "girls" (or *chickies* or *Sheilas*) and to be excluded from decision-making discussions. However, they do receive maternity benefits, have access to their husbands' pension funds (even after divorce), and don't automatically gain custody of the children.

Some Gains

A recent poll by Johannesburg's *Business Day* newspaper found that 53 percent of women believe that gender prejudice in the private sector remains unchecked. Statistical and anecdotal evidence of this bias abounds. As for the notion of sexual harassment in the workplace — one female sales representative says she's propositioned on about one in ten sales calls and receives no sympathy from her boss who, in fact, has hinted that sleeping with select customers would be good for business. When asked why she just doesn't leave the company, her reply is that it wouldn't be any better elsewhere.

In 1997, women comprised 2 percent of board members within South Africa's top 1,000 companies. While this pales in comparison to the U.S. (83 percent of Fortune 500 companies have female representation on their boards), it's still an improvement over 1995, when just 0.5 percent of South Africa's top 1,000 firms had a woman in the boardroom. (It's important to consider, however, that few South African women between the ages of thirty and fifty have had the benefit of a university education.) Women now make up 41 percent of the country's workforce, yet they receive, on average, just 50 percent of their male counterparts' pay.

Nelson Mandela's government has formally introduced a series of gender equality laws meant to redress discrimination, but legislating away a national mind-set and centuries of tradition is easier said than done. The presence of multinational companies, complete with their imported view of gender equality and equal pay for equal work, has so far been the biggest contributing factor to shattering the "glass ceiling" for females.

Women, especially white females, must take some of the blame for the relatively slow pace of change. Many still believe that creating a traditional family is the chief goal of womanhood. Work fills the time until Prince Charming comes along. Having a career never occurs to them.

Dealing with Macho Men

Foreign businesswomen can expect to run into a condescending attitude at virtually every level in both the black and white cultures. Rank or title don't automatically gain women respect, as they often do for men. Expect to be tested. Remarks, including sexual innuendo, may be aimed at provoking a reaction or simply uttered for shock value. A thick skin is required, at least in the initial phase. Take the remarks, including compliments about appearance, in stride and move onto the next point. South Africans admire toughness, confidence and competence, but like sharks circling a kill, they'll pounce if they

BAKER COLLEGE OF MUSKEGON LIBRARY
MUSKEGON, MICHIGAN 49442

perceive weakness. Regardless of the provocation, refrain from giving a lecture on political correctness. It may put an end to any deals in progress.

"The first few days of negotiations were brutal," recalls a female American attorney who was in Johannesburg to close a multimillion dollar manufacturing deal. "The South Africans involved just kept talking right past me to the male members of my team. It was distracting for me. I couldn't focus, I was so enraged." Finally, she says, she earned their respect by demonstrating her legal expertise and being a tough, unflustered negotiator. "When I said 'no,' it meant no and they seemed to understand that. Suddenly, they started talking to me like, if you'll excuse the expression, like I was one of the guys. I think if I had 'lost my cool' early on, we would have blown the deal." She says one key to her success was the support of the males on her negotiating team, who reinforced her authority as team leader. "Without that," she says, "it would have taken me so much longer to get them to listen to and respect me."

If it comes naturally a little harmless flirtation (if there is such a thing) can go a long way. South African males have such large egos that "playing up to them" can be an instant ice breaker. Trying to be asexual will not get you very far very fast, nor will it help your business or win you respect.

8   Making Connections

An Elitist Road

South Africa's white, English-speaking business elite generally share similar backgrounds — private schools and one of the top three local universities or *varsities,* as they're known, with a dash of overseas experience and military service (no longer compulsory) thrown in. The Afrikaans business elite have traveled the same route, but through Afrikaner schools.

The current black business elite have traveled yet a third road, more akin to "the college of hard knocks." Many were involved either internally or in exile with the liberation movement (the ANC) and many, such as Deputy President Thabo Mbeki, have earned post-graduate degrees overseas. Often, the leading African businessmen have much more foreign living experiences (forced into exile by the white minority government) than their white counterparts.

Still, this is a relatively small community. English and Afrikaners have known and competed against each other on the sports fields and in the executive suite for decades. It's the quintessential

Old Boys' Network and a tough nut to crack for outsiders. South Africans appreciate "good breeding" and tend to be snobs about education. An advanced degree from Harvard or the Sorbonne will impress the hell out of them.

Introductions & Middlemen

Preliminary telephone calls and faxes will take you only so far when it comes to building a business relationship. (Cellular phone service was introduced in 1994.) Letters of introduction, if coming from someone well known to the person you intend to do business with, will carry more weight here than in most other countries.

Because the business community is so incestuous (and to some extent, elitist), using a middleman to handle introductions isn't a particularly useful approach, at least in the white community. There's no real history of appreciating the role of middlemen in business here. Less than 50 percent of total merchandise sales pass through a wholesaler. Most business is conducted directly between the manufacturer and the retailer.

Foreigners should consider contacting chambers of commerce, consulate commercial services, trade commissions or embassies in their native countries in order to establish initial contacts. When scheduling appointments from abroad, do so a month or two in advance, if possible, and avoid summer (everything shuts down between mid-December through mid-January), the week before Easter, and, to a lesser extent, major Jewish holidays (Johannesburg has a sizable Jewish community).

9   Strategies for Success

Do They Need You?

South Africans have an enormous amount of national pride. While the Holy Grail for many small- and medium-sized businesses is an overseas partner, don't expect them to prostitute themselves to get one. Many feel that the domestic market is indeed large enough to make a comfortable living in, that entry into the southern African regional exporting market is all they need to make it big, and that they can do so without outside help. Decades of international sanctions have taught South African businesses to be self-reliant. While overseas investors may represent access to capital, it's not a given that local businesses want foreign advice.

Ten Keys to Business Success

- **Build relationships.** You can telephone and fax and e-mail all you want but South Africans are reluctant to deal with anyone they haven't met face-to-face. Business is about friends and colleagues; "the bottom line" comes second. A South African would rather do so-so business with a friend than good business with a stranger. Establishing a strong personal relationship means trust, and trust will move a deal along much more quickly than sweetening the pot with extra cash.

- **Think big.** Since the end of apartheid, the most successful deals in South Africa have been export-oriented. Any deal should include some provision for the export of goods at least to neighboring African states. Think big. The fact that the world has recently opened itself to South African commerce is a great lure to local businesses. They want partners who can lead them to the promised land of global exports.

- **Be patient.** It really isn't in the nature of South Africans to drive hard bargains or quibble over price and detail. Time moves relatively slowly here. Cracking down or being overly aggressive about deadlines or the pace of decisionmaking will probably not hasten the process along. Instead, such tactics will poison your personal relationship.

- **Stick to your deal.** Many deals are still sealed with a handshake (though it's becoming increasingly important to get things in writing). Those who renege on a bargain are unlikely to get a second chance. The business community is incestuous and fairly small. Once a foreign firm earns a reputation as a deal breaker, reviving its image will be an arduous and timeconsuming task.

- **Exchange controls**. In an era of government currency exchange control regulations, doing business overseas is rife with difficulties. Deals that help foreign exchange issues and are creative in their funding will be most interesting to South Africans. Coming into talks with a good understanding and strategy on how to handle the bane of South African commerce can make all the difference. As of July 1997, such restrictions on individual investment have been relaxed, but they remain in place for corporate structures.

- **Embrace affirmative action.** Black participation in the economy is a national obsession at present, encouraged by both the private and government sectors. Be prepared to discuss ways of managing affirmative action (South Africans prefer the term "equal opportunity issues") and have practical tips on handling racial integration in the workplace. Providing practical guidelines to compliance without hurting company performance and morale are highly valued here. But please, no lectures on the morality of affirmative action.

  A strong affirmative action program can set you apart from most competitors. Training and education are two other buzz words that many South African businesses (especially black-owned ones) listen for in contract talks.

- **Be aware of your own prejudices.** Yes, there are differences between South Africa's black and white cultures, but don't be fooled into thinking that they're vast within the business community. African businessmen get frustrated when black stereotypes are applied to them. Any uneasiness about race (however subtle) or a patronizing attitude will kill a deal before it starts.

- **Understand the political climate.** When operating within the black business community, try to understand the mind-set of an excluded majority. They got most of their support in the liberation struggle from the USSR, China and other communist countries, while for an extended period, the white-minority government they were fighting enjoyed support from Western nations. Showing understanding and sensitivity toward this issue will demonstrate a sincerity of purpose on your part. Don't expect them to fawn all over you because you're from the West. You were, after all, closely associated with the enemy at one time.

- **Choose a local partner with care**. In many ways, a black partner is vital, but don't be seduced into a relationship with a nonperforming person who claims to have the right connections. Look for a partner who can bring together all the necessary elements for your business, regardless of his or her cultural or ethnic group.

- **Know the law.** South African corporate law, like its tax system, is an unforgiving maze of corporate structures, each of which has distinct advantages and disadvantages. Before seeking out a partner or beginning talks, have some idea of which legal structure will work best for your business.

Business Gifts

Though not mandatory, a small thoughtful gift for business associates or their families will be greatly appreciated — *after* developing a relationship. Your gift should be personalized, somehow. A high-quality pen or a dozen golf balls with an individual's name and company logo printed on them would be considered by many to be perfect gestures.

10 Time

Time: It Depends

There are definite differences in the approach to time between white and black cultures in South Africa. Whites, while not exactly slaves to the clock, are less casual than their black counterparts. Still, compared to the rest of Africa and owing to the high degree of international contact that South Africans businesses have, the concept of time is decidedly Western.

Expect to be kept waiting five out of ten times for formal appointments at any level (you'll inevitably be served a cup of tea or coffee.) Last-minute cancellations are routine, especially with the advent of the mobile telephone. Visitors can often judge their importance by the amount of time they're kept waiting before a scheduled meeting. The longer the wait, the lower they are on the food chain.

The bigger the company and the more formal the structure, the more likely it is that meetings will begin and end on time. A visiting American journalist was amazed when his series of interviews with senior executives at Anglo American (the giant mining and manufacturing conglomerate based in Johannesburg) went off with military precision, seemingly timed to the minute.

The conundrum facing visiting businesspeople is that while they can expect most meetings to begin late, it can be fatal to fail to show up at the appointed time. Expect no quarter. A British businessman reports being ten minutes late for a planned one hour meeting at Anglo American. The executive refused to see him even though the time had already been allocated. His secretary apologized but explained that her boss had certain standards.

At smaller companies, especially black-owned ones, the approach to time is highly casual. Showing impatience or snapping at the receptionist or secretary is counterproductive. There's little they can do to speed things along. It's wise to ask if it would be better to reschedule for another day; it could save you hours of waiting time. An executive may be unable to show up for a noon appointment until 4 P.M., but you won't be told this unless you ask.

Avoid scheduling your appointments too closely together. And it's important to leave a local contact number with those you're planning to see, so that you can be contacted in the event of time changes or cancellations. Always call a day in advance or even the same day to reconfirm. It will spare you having to spend sunny afternoons waiting in empty offices while your contact is enjoying one of those fabled multiple-martini lunches (see Chapter 20) in which time seems to stand still.

Appointments

Because of the inordinate amount of domestic and international travel done by many South African executives, appointments should be scheduled as far in advance as possible. A month is an adequate cushion, and even then, you'll probably not garner anywhere near a 100 percent success rate. Getting all the ducks lined up in a row is difficult. The odds of getting an appointment with a senior executive with only a week's notice are extremely slim. However, mentioning that you'll be coming from overseas and have only a limited time to spend in the country will help somewhat.

Deadlines

The approach to deadlines is rather casual, even in a country as relatively efficient as South Africa. "I told one small manufacturer I was working with that we had an absolute 'drop dead' deadline for his materials in two weeks. His reply was he wanted to know where the funeral was going to be," says an American exporter working in South Africa.

If you must impose strict deadlines, spell them out clearly and write them into the contract. The best advice? Allow a couple of weeks as a cushion. When you ask a South African to do something, you're likely to hear one of two responses which, though similar in sound, are as different as night and day. One is, "I will do it now-now." The other is, "I will do it just now." *Now-now* carries a sense of immediacy; it means a task has been given top priority. *Just now* is the South African equivalent of *mañana*. It means that a task has low priority and will get done some time in the unspecified future — maybe.

11 Business Meetings

Arranging the Meeting: Half the Battle

Since apartheid ended, businesses have flocked here in the hope of turning a buck or *yen* with little knowledge of how business works, and South African senior executives have grown somewhat leery of this approach. Big business is more sophisticated here than many think. Don't expect to arrange meetings without an amount of long-distance telephone and fax contact beforehand — much of it one way. South Africans believe that they have much to offer and that they should be pursued.

Any initial request for a face-to-face meeting should include as many specifics as possible about your company, your own qualifications (and those of colleagues who'll be attending the meeting) and an outline of what you're proposing. Experience in dealing in the developing world is considered a plus, as are any references from other companies you've dealt with or press clips that help legitimize your firm's international or domestic standing.

Enough advance time should be allotted to ensure that the person you want to see will be avail-

able. Not wishing to disappoint the overseas businessman, secretaries and personnel assistants will
often suggest someone else to meet with in the corporation if their boss isn't available. This can lead to
a wasted trip. If you've firmly identified who you
should be meeting, stick to your guns. Any substitute will probably have no decision-making responsibilities or ownership of the proposed project or
venture. Alter your schedule, if necessary.

Preparing for the Meeting

Any hint of ignorance about the domestic or
regional political scene will almost immediately dis-
qualify you from doing business in this country.
Generic ideas don't work here, especially when it
comes to financing and foreign exchange. Foreigners
are expected to know the obstacles going in; South
Africans don't want to spend time explaining them.
Rather, it's the foreign businessperson who should
be offering solutions. There's no substitute for doing
your homework in advance of any meeting, especially when it comes to exchange controls and profit
repatriation.

Arriving at the Company

Often, larger companies will offer to send a
driver to your hotel to pick you up, or to take you
back afterward. When possible, sit in the back seat.
Tipping isn't required, but a gift (like a company
pen) would be a nice gesture and it will probably
win you a friend. If driving to a meeting yourself,
allow plenty of time. The address system, especially
in the suburbs, seems to follow no known logical
pattern, and many times the addresses are impossible to see from the street. In the city, finding secure
parking may be next to impossible.

At most large corporations, you'll be asked on arrival to sign a visitor's book and will be given an identity badge that must be surrendered when you leave the building. You'll almost never be sent up to an office unattended. The person at the front reception desk will telephone upstairs to a secretary or personal assistant, who fetches you in the lobby and escorts you to the meeting. He or she will also escort you out of the building when your meeting is over.

Once you arrive on the proper floor, you'll be asked if you want coffee or tea. This seems to be an ice breaker and often leads to interesting conversation, which you can use to learn the latest about the company you're dealing with while waiting for your meeting. Also, developing a personal relationship with a secretary can be a key for obtaining a second meeting. Secretaries have enormous power over their bosses' meeting schedules.

The Meeting Begins

Introductions are usually done in order of seniority. Exchanging business cards is normally done at the start of a meeting. It's okay to glance at a card you've been given. Always wait to be asked to sit down; once seated, expect to be asked yet again if you want coffee or tea. It's a good idea to except, as this provides a break in the formality and allows for the start of personal conversation.

South Africans aren't big on slide presentations or overhead projectors. The first meeting is about establishing a personal rapport and determining if you're a person they can trust. Once this judgment is made, the nitty gritty details can be dealt with. Don't expect any snap judgments or instant deals. Everything will be taken under advisement.

Guidelines for Conducting a Meeting

- Keep it short, crisp and loaded with specific ideas that deal with the special circumstances of doing business in South Africa. Sometimes, the logistics and financing of the deal are more important to South Africans than the actual product or service you're selling.
- Personalize whenever possible. Deals are built on trust, and striking a personal chord will enhance your chances. Casually mentioning that you'd love to see a cricket match or rugby game might just get you an invitation to one (South Africans love to explain the intricacies of their national sports) and offer a great opportunity to cultivate a business relationship.
- Don't hard sell. Nothing is more off-putting to a South African executive than someone who's too pushy. Business isn't done that way.

Concluding the Meeting

Since it's considered rude to interrupt a speaker, you need to ask at the conclusion of your meeting if there are questions about your presentation or your company. Don't leave the follow-up in the hands of the South Africans. Rather, tell them when you intend to make the next contact, even if they offer to get back to you first. If the person you're meeting with should decide to escort you personally down to the outer lobby, take advantage of this time to broach such non-business subjects as sports, food, family or entertainment. This is truly a prime relationship-building opportunity. Business deals can be won or lost during the time it takes to ride an elevator down twelve stories.

12 Negotiating with South Africans

Avoid Pressure Tactics

Negotiations generally begin with a round of handshakes and small talk during which foreign businesspeople will be sized up as to their local knowledge, their sense of humor and their eagerness to complete a deal. Negotiations are conducted here as they are in the West, with a few subtle differences. South Africans will not allow anyone to con them, bully them or pressure them into making a less-than-thoroughly-thought-out business decision. A British colleague tells how, frustrated by the slow pace of the decision-making process, he requested a meeting and then informed his South African counterparts that he needed a decision on his proposal within 24 hours. The reply was simply, "That's impossible."

"I backed myself into a corner out of frustration and I paid for it. We eventually got the order, but it probably took a few weeks longer because I tried to force the issue. They saw right through me." Knowing that Westerners, particularly Americans, seem to work under tough but artificial time constraints, South Africans will often use a deliberately slow pace to win additional concessions.

Turn Down the Volume

Discussions should be conducted in a friendly manner and in quiet voices. Leave the shouting for the rugby match, it doesn't impress anyone. A raised voice is actually counterproductive, it will be taken as a personal insult. Plus, it runs the risk of getting you branded as an obsessive foreigner more concerned about "the bottom line" than the relationships of business.

Basically, it's safe to get down to business and be firm, but without being gratuitously aggressive. An ultimatum should be used only as a last resort. If it fails to draw an immediate and sincere reaction, walk away. The deal is over.

Personalize the Talks

The ability to relate to the person you're negotiating with is vitally important. Deals are made on a personal level, not on a corporate one, and for a deal to be successfully concluded, the negotiators must end up as friends. Sport chat is a great ice breaker. Bone up on the country's accomplishments in golf, rugby and cricket. Don't initiate or be drawn into racist or sexist conversations. Save such topics for after-hours, once you get to know your South African contact better. And even then, listen rather than lecture.

Win-Win

South Africans aren't cut-throat negotiators. Rather, they seek to build consensus and would prefer to see all sides gain something. For the most part, they're ruled by a sense of fair play, and it's contrary to their nature to haggle over price or quibble over details. Try to present a win-win situation in talks, rather than offering choices that limit the proceedings to a win-lose format.

Often, South Africans believe that foreigners need them more than they need foreign business. It's worth mentioning, without making a grand point of it, that you've explored other options and approached other companies about the business at hand. But don't bluff. The Old Boys' Network provides good feedback, and getting caught out in a lie or a half truth will poison the atmosphere, possibly for good.

One mention about note taking: It's rare at negotiating sessions. When notes *are* taken, a secretary will do it. For the principals to do so would demean their status.

Inexperience

Many of South Africa's smaller or mid-sized firms, both black and white, lack experience dealing internationally, and they may overestimate their capability to meet your requirements. Don't leave things vague. Clearly enumerate the expected performance standards and time requirements, and the penalties for failing to meet them. For many South Africans, the details are a bore. It's up to the foreign counterpart to spell out responsibilities if future problems and disappointments are to be avoided.

Contracts

South Africa isn't a litigious society. Business contracts tend to follow the pattern of those drawn up in Britain and continental Europe. They're not overly complicated, but they're sometimes worded in a vague manner intentionally to give the local party some "wiggle room," should things not work out. The South African legal system is fair and mostly devoid of corruption, but it does seem to favor the local side over the foreign side in cases of corporate and business law.

Interpreters

As one English-speaking European business-man put it, "If you need to use an interpreter in South Africa, you're either trying to negotiate for a herd of cattle or you're in the wrong country." English *is* spoken in business circles, though on occasion, some Afrikaans businessmen may suggest the use of an interpreter as protection during sensitive contract talks with foreigners.

The quality of non-European language skills among locals remains dubious. If you speak Dutch, you'll be able to converse in Afrikaans. If you intend to use an interpreter, notify your host in advance as a courtesy. Finding a skilled local linguist who speaks Spanish, Italian, German, Japanese, Chinese or even French may take considerable time. Consider paying the expense of bringing your own.

Having to use an interpreter is a considerable disadvantage in South Africa because of the emphasis on personal contact, relationship building and after-hours flings.

13   Business Outside the Law

Though the country's official unemployment rate is in excess of 35 percent, many economists believe it to be substantially lower due to a proliferating underground economy. Because blacks were restricted in commerce under apartheid (for example, there are no supermarkets in black townships because apartheid laws limited the size of retail space an African was allowed to own or operate), many took to opening businesses "off the books," escaping taxes and government regulation. Though apartheid ended, the tradition did not.

Smuggling hit its stride during the 1870s and 1880s; diamonds were hidden in cigarettes and hollow shoe-heels, and even wrapped in meat and fed to hungry dogs. Today, with the opening of the country's borders to neighboring African states, the smuggling of goods (textiles, shoes, sports equipment, radios) to avoid the 14 percent VAT has exploded, while attracting some rather unsavory but experienced black marketeers from West Africa. Still, compared with most other African nations, South Africa is a land of plenty with every type of consumer good readily available. Counterfeit goods and knockoffs are prevalent in hawker stalls.

Car Theft

Incidents of carjacking have exploded in recent years (they jumped more than 12 percent in 1996 to 8,524 in Johannesburg alone), with sophisticated international rings responsible for much of the rise. Some drivers are stopped at red lights and ordered out at gunpoint. Those vehicles that aren't victims of the efficient "chop shops" that hack up vehicles for parts usually end up in neighboring African countries. Prime landing areas are the "killer Zs" — Zambia and Zimbabwe. As a result, auto insurance rates, especially for rental vehicles, are prohibitive. For security reasons, consider hiring a car with a driver. Taxis can be hired by the hour or by the day and half day, but negotiate a rate beforehand. Though many have meters, they rarely seem to be turned on.

Crime: Rampant & Increasingly Organized

South Africa is home to one of the highest per capita murder rates in the world, about six times that of the U.S., or what amounts to some 70 murders every day. Several studies have estimated the economic cost of street and white-collar crime to be in excess of 41 billion *rand* (US$10 billion) annually, the equivalent of the GNP of some smaller African states. Eighty percent of all South Africa households reported having experienced a crime against person or property within a two-year period. Predictably, no less than 71 percent of the populace wants to reinstate the death penalty, which was only abolished in 1995.

Crime is also becoming increasingly organized. Police estimate that there are more than 450 organized crime syndicates operating within South Africa, including arms of the Russian Mafia and of South American drug cartels.

Under apartheid, the country was considered "safer," but few benefited and economic growth slowed to a standstill. Increased political freedom brought with it IBM, Ford, General Motors, and hope for a better future. True, freedom also brought an increase in crime in white areas, but relative to the rest of the continent, South Africa is no worse off than Nairobi and probably a lot safer than Lagos.

Baksheshis & Petty Bribery

By the standards of a continent that has suffered under the weight of official corruption, South Africa is remarkably corruption free. President Mandela's African National Congress remains remarkably untainted by major scandal, though there are signs that kickbacks for government tenders, especially from local contractors and companies, are becoming more common.

Small-scale bribery is growing among police and some local-level officials when it comes to circumventing minor infractions of the law. To many South Africans, this is a worrisome trend. Kickbacks (*baksheshis*) among locals are rampant.

The previous white government set the tone. Prime Minister John Vorster was brought down by a corruption and influence-peddling scandal that included attempts to purchase the now-defunct *Washington Star* newspaper with a secret, government propaganda slush fund. Petty bribery was as rife in the white-run civil service as it's now in the increasingly black-run civil service. In fact, white collar crime is soaring, and much of it is being committed by white managers. Up to 60 percent of all fraud cases in the country are orchestrated by the management of legitimate companies.

All that having been said, few international businesspeople have reported encountering blatant demands for bribes or a piece of the action (not uncommon in other African nations). Don't act hastily if approached. A firm but polite "We don't do business that way" may suffice.

Drugs & Money Laundering

The smoking of *dagga* (marijuana) has long been a national pastime in both black and white circles, despite the extremely harsh penalties for possession and dealing that existed under conservative, white government rule. The coastal region of Natal provided prime growing areas of *dagga*. "Durban Poison" (as one cultivar was known) was famous throughout Africa for its near-mystical highs. But as the country's borders have opened up and the jobless have migrated from black townships into the city, harder drugs (particularly cocaine and even crack) have become more prevalent.

Johannesburg's once-fashionable cafe district and Hillbrow's pleasant residential hotels have turned into drug markets and crack houses run mostly by immigrants from West Africa. With its excellent international airline and maritime connections, South Africa has become a major transit point for cocaine and heroin bound from Asia and North Africa for Europe and North America.

Dealing on the streets has become blatant. One American journalist says he witnessed the sale of cocaine on a Hillbrow street corner in broad daylight, while a half block away a traffic cop was busy writing parking tickets, occasionally looking up to take in the drug transaction a few yards away but taking no action.

So at a loss is the police force that it called in an American business consulting group to reorganize its stations. Another reason for the booming drug trade is the country's highly sophisticated and almost-no-questions-asked banking system, which has become a popular money-laundering station for world drug cartels from South America and West Africa.

Prostitution: The Calvinist Backlash

South Africa's prudishness under white Afrikanerdom has given way to a booming sex industry, complete with classy bordellos, a large contingent of eastern European madams, and street-walking prostitutes of all colors and nationalities. Though prostitution is illegal, newspapers are rife with advertisements for sex services of every description. The country that once banned lingerie catalogues as smut and routinely confiscated *Sports Illustrated*'s annual swimsuit issue at airport customs on the grounds that it was pornographic now boasts its own soft porn magazines, including one published in Afrikaans entitled *Loslyf* (Loose Life).

What began as an almost quaint loss of national innocence has evolved into something decidedly ugly. South Africa now rivals Thailand and the Philippines as a center for child prostitution and pedophilia. So-called township taxi queens — black preteen prostitutes — thrive in the major cities. Not coincidentally, statistics sight children and teenagers as being seven times more likely to be the victims of rape than adult females. The AIDS epidemic that's hitting South Africa hard seems to be of little deterrence to the sex industry here.

14   Names & Greetings

And So, How is Your Family Today?

The English, the Afrikaners and the black Africans all have distinct forms of greeting, and each tends to mirror their collective personality. Expect what sounds like a rather clipped *Mora, meneer* (literally, Morning, mister) from the Afrikaners. While it sounds less than warm, it's about as informal as it gets until you develop a personal relationship.

English-speaking white South Africans follow the British style of a formal exchange of pleasantries, not overly sincere but polite. Everybody, but everybody shakes hands.

Black South Africans are far less structured in their greetings (a function of a less manic outlook on time). Expect to be asked how your trip was and how your family is doing. The tradition of long greetings stems from a time when Africans walked miles to visit neighboring villages on social calls. A gushing greeting was considered the least a villager could do for the traveler. Don't be impatient with such long drawn-out exchanges. Rather, get into the spirit and appreciate that the person you came to see is prepared to take the time to sincerely inquire about your welfare.

Names & Titles

English-speaking white South Africans seem big on double-barreled hyphenated last names like Brown-Smyth. In formal correspondence, they'll often use initials followed by their surname, as in P. J. Brown-Smyth. Afrikaans family names are slightly more complicated and frequently include a lower-case prefix, e.g., Jan van der Merwe.

It's often easy to identify an African's ethnic or tribal origin by his or her surname. Most Africans will have several given names, which may include an English or Afrikaans name, a biblical name, plus another from his or her ethnic group. However, for business purposes, they're usually shortened to a given name and a surname. Be aware that because African names tend to be mellifluous, they can grate when a foreigner mispronounces them.

Generally speaking, titles such as *Doctor* aren't used in business or academic circles, though some businessmen with honorary doctorates will insist on being addressed in this manner. On occasion, African businesspeople will, in conversation, use one's surname only ("Tell me, Smyth, what do you think of ..."). This isn't meant to be rude or challenging, rather it's a sign of a personal warming and the start of a relationship.

Avoid using the term *Miss* or the Afrikaans equivalent *mejuffrou* in business conversations. They've developed a pejorative connotation, something more akin to *missy*. When in doubt as to a female's marital status, leave it out.

Company Names: An Alphabet Soup

Corporations like to refer to themselves with an alphabet soup of initials that identify their structure and legal standing. *Ltd.* (an abbreviation for Limited) or in Afrikaans *Bpk.* are roughly the equivalent of *Incorporated* in U.S. terms, and they generally signify a publicly traded company. Smaller companies will refer to themselves as *PTY. LTD* (in Afrikaans, *Edms. Bpk*). This generally refers to a privately held company, though it can also indicate a wholly owned subsidiary of a public company.

The Employer/Employee Relationship

This is probably the hardest relationship for a foreigner to adapt to in South Africa. Yes, it's okay to address drivers, cleaners, tea ladies, housemaids, cooks and lift operators by their first name, as long as it's done respectfully. However, expect to be called by your last name with a title such as *Mr.*, *Mrs.* or *Miss* by people employed in the service industry.

"I could tell there was something bothering Margaret, my housemaid, for weeks, but I couldn't put my finger on it," recalls an American lawyer who was residing in South Africa. "She seemed eager to avoid me and rarely spoke. I just couldn't figure it." After cornering Margaret in the kitchen one afternoon, the lawyer discovered the source of her maid's unhappiness. Weeks before, the lawyer had instructed Margaret to call her by her first name, Catherine. "It seems Margaret couldn't handle it. She was so uncomfortable with it, she just avoided talking to me." The solution: Margaret reverted to addressing her employer by her last name and title.

It may take some getting used to, but when in Rome — or Pretoria, for that matter — do what the locals do.

Communication Styles

Let's Get Physical

South Africans are warm and friendly people by nature, and conversation can get very personnel very quickly. There's a genuine interest in how foreigners live and how they view South Africa. Small talk reigns.

South Africans like to be physical when talking. There's a lot of handshaking and backslapping (and in the case of black Africans, handholding is a sign of friendship). This is a macho world and a firm handshake is an important first line of communication for any person, male or female, wishing to make an impression. (The "African handshake," a handshake augmented by slipping a free hand around the other person's thumb, is used between blacks and whites and between blacks, but not between whites.) Eye contact is essential. Also, be prepared for the inevitable sports analogies. In this sports-mad country, it seems that every business situation can be compared to a game of cricket, soccer or rugby. When passing through a doorway, it's customary for African men to precede women.

Not the Queen's English

English is, by and large, politically neutral and the language of commerce. Because of its association with U.S. pop culture, it's especially fashionable among black youth. But South African English, like American English, has peculiarities that make it unrecognizable to someone who speaks the Queen's version.

When a business colleague offers to give you a *tinkle*, he's talking about a telephone call. The expression *ag shame* can mean "How cute" (as when one compliments the parents of a young baby); it can also be used to express sympathy (as in "What a shame"). *Jawellnofine*; a combination of the words *yes*, *well*, *no* and *fine*, means something akin to, "What do you want me to do about it?" Whole dictionaries have been written about fractured South African English, a language in which *no* sometimes means *yes* or nothing at all. Ask a South African how he is and you'll likely get the response "No, I'm fine."

One practice visitors may find annoying is hearing a lengthy joke told in English, only to have the punch line delivered in Afrikaans, simply because it sounds funnier.

Many Afrikaans expressions have been adapted into the everyday English vocabulary of South Africans, such as *lekker* (good or nice) and *bakkie* (pick-up truck). No one is quite sure about the origin of *babbelas* (pronounced bob-el-ass), which is roughly the equivalent of a hangover.

Some other everyday South Africanisms:

- **Café** (pronounced Kaf). A café or a corner grocery store.
- **Bell.** Used either as a noun or a verb. "Give me a *bell* in the morning" means "Telephone me"; "I'll *bell* you" means "I'll call you."

- **Strusbob.** This is a form of punctuation used when a speaker expects a listener to be skeptical. For example: "I went to the casino last week and won 1,000 *rand, strusbob*." The word seems to be bastardization of "True as God."

- **Dop.** A cocktail or drink. "Let's go for a *dop* later."

- **Platteland.** Refers to unsophisticated, conservative rural areas. "Will this play in the *Platteland*?" is the equivalent of "Will it play in Peoria?"

- **Donner.** Literally "thunder" in Afrikaans, it's used as slang to mean a severe beating, as in "I'm going to *donner* you" or "My team got *donnered* in the last game."

Age = Wisdom

In African cultures, there's great respect for ancestors as well as elders, who are seen as repositories of experience and the wisdom that comes with it. To not show the proper respect to someone who is your elder is highly offensive to most Africans. While urbanization appears to be leading to a breakdown of these traditions, they remain strong in rural areas.

A Desire To Not Disappoint

Black South Africans initially tend to be more reserved in their business communication style than their white counterparts, that is, until a relationship develops and the physical side takes over. Then, Africans are even bigger huggers and back-slappers than whites. Many will speak English with a heavy accent, as well as in a rapid cadence. Pay attention. Asking for constant repeats will eventually be deemed insulting. And avoid replying in anything but your normal tone, volume and pace. Speaking more slowly, along the lines of the Voice of America's Special English News broadcast, will also insult your listener. South Africans may *speak* with an accent, but they don't *listen* with one.

And they don't like to admit that they don't know an answer. It ties in with the tradition of hospitality and the desire to not disappoint. If you ask a question that can't be answered, expect an answer anyway. The correct information will be forwarded to you, one way or another, during subsequent contacts.

Guidelines for Foreigners

- **Maintain your sense of humor.** Humor, often self-deprecating, is as common as gazelles are in the Kruger National Park. South Africans expect you to laugh with them, and even sometimes *at* them, as long as they too are laughing.
- **Be physical.** Shying away from physical contact may be interpreted as aloofness, unfriendliness, or a lack of trust.
- **Don't interrupt.** Interrupting a speaker in midsentence to make a point will draw, if not an "Excuse me, now let me continue" rebuke, then at least an admonishing stare.
- **Positive reinforcement.** This seems to put South Africans at ease. If you're listening, it's to your advantage to nod in agreement and to occasionally agree verbally as well.

16   Customs

Changing Sensibilities: From Covenant to Reconciliation

Determined to not repeat the mistakes of the white minority government (that is, shoving one particular culture and morality down people's throats), the ANC has adopted two national anthems: *Nkosi Sikelel' iAfrika* (God Bless Africa), the anthem of the anti-apartheid liberation movement and *Die Stem* (The Call of South Africa), the Afrikaner-inspired anthem of apartheid days. Both are sung at official functions and sporting events.

Another dramatic change is the de-emphasis on what was formerly called the Day of the Covenant (December 16). One of the greatest Afrikaans folk heroes is Andries Pretorious, who led a ragtag force of 500 Afrikaners to victory over 10,000 "heathen" Zulu *impis* (warriors) in the Battle of Blood River in 1838. December 16th marked this victory, which the Afrikaners claimed was part of a divine covenant with God that confirmed their superiority over blacks and underscored their divine right to rule.

It was truly the Afrikaner national holiday — as solemn and holy as Good Friday and a constant reminder to blacks of their second-class status. Celebrations centered on the Voortrekker (Pioneer) Monument near Pretoria, where whites would dress in period costume and re-enact their military triumph. Rather than eliminate the holiday entirely, the government changed its name to the Day of Reconciliation and its focus to one of national racial harmony. Afrikaners still celebrate it as they have in the past, but the crowds — and the angst — have lessened.

Christmas

Christmas is the most important holiday for blacks and whites. Though it falls in the summer, South Africans try to approximate the fuzzy warmth of wintertime, including somewhat traditional Western holiday foods. "I simply couldn't get over the fake snow and plastic reindeer everywhere," says one British resident. He was relieved, however, to find that when he went to rent a Father Christmas suit for a party, he had a choice of shorts or long pants to go with the bushy beard and woolen cap.

Music & Dance

Music and dance have always been integral to African culture, whether to a courtship, a marriage, a funeral, the preparation for a hunt, or even the anti-apartheid liberation struggle. The traditional *toi-toi* or "liberation dance of the people" was adapted to the modern-day fight against apartheid in the black townships. Uniquely black South African music forms include *mapantsula* (better know as township jive), a cross between early rap and traditional jazz, and *isicatamiya*, a usually mournful choir or choral group that had its beginnings in the gold mines (where black migrant laborers lived, forcibly separated from their families for months on end).

While the country remains basically European in orientation, whites have long taken some of the best in African theater, music and dance and blended it with their own to establish a truly unique Euro-African mix.

Tribal Traditions

All of South Africa's cultures have rich traditions, some of which are disappearing. Among the Zulu, beads play an important role during courtship. They're strung into ornaments (waistbands, necklaces) whose colors and patterns can convey complex messages. ("I am in love with you" [white], "but there are difficulties" [black] "because you lack cattle dowry" [pink]. "Therefore I feel weak and sickly" [green].) Among several tribes, including the Xhosa, male circumcision remains an important rite of passage between boyhood and manhood. Ndebele traditions include the wearing of *iindzila* (stacked brass and copper rings) by married women on their ankles, arms and neck, and painting the exterior of their homes with colorful, elaborate geometric designs.

When invited to the home of a Zulu, it's polite to shout from the gate that you've arrived, but when you walk into the home, it's rude to make yourself comfortable without first being seated by the host. In contrast, in the Sotho culture, once invited into the home you're expected to sit down immediately; the hosts will arrange themselves around you. If it's clear that foreigners are making an attempt to understand (and aren't being patronizing), Africans will be immediately welcoming. In most cases, African cultures are more respectful of the individual than Western cultures.

Sport: A National Obsession

Soccer (called football here) is the most popular sport in the black community. There are more than 15,000 registered soccer clubs here and more than one million active players. One of the larger scandals to rock the government recently was an allegation that Deputy President Thabo Mbeki was late arriving for an international soccer match against Brazil, delaying the start of the game by fifteen minutes. Rugby is played by Afrikaners, while South African English prefer cricket. Basketball, once the exclusive domain of the more recent immigrant communities such as the Portuguese and the Greeks, has spread to the black community with a vengeance. Tennis, golf, surfing, squash and field hockey are also popular.

After decades of isolation, the country lives and dies according to the fortunes of its teams. South Africans will admit that of all the sanctions imposed during the apartheid years, it was the ban from international sporting competitions that psychologically hurt them most.

Sport has proven to be a great unifier, one of the few areas in which the races can compete with equality. In a pub recently, watching the South African national soccer team (nicknamed *Bifana*, "The Boys") defeat Australia in an international tournament, each goal elicited hugs and back slaps between blacks and whites. Hopefully, such a scene is a glimpse of the future.

17   Dress & Appearance

Conservative is Best

It's safe to say that South Africa isn't one of the fashion meccas of the world. Style is defined by simple (if sometimes frumpish) elegance and is more Western than it is African — with American-style jeans, T-shirts and *takkies* (sneakers) popular in the poorer black urban areas. Save the safari suit and bush hat for your visit to the game park, though even there, you'll be instantly spotted as a tourist. Only game rangers wear and actually look good in that kind of outfit. And void the urge to "go native." Nothing looks sillier than a sun-deprived foreigner in a *dashiki* in the middle of a metropolis the size of Johannesburg or Durban. You may as well wear a "please mug me" sign on your forehead.

Global business travelers should opt for conservative, preferably tropical weight, suits. A white or light-colored dress shirt and a tie are standard. Long sleeve shirts are preferred. Short sleeves are best reserved for after-work casual meetings. In rural communities, women should avoid wearing sleeveless, low-cut or otherwise revealing garments. Keep in mind that winter falls between June and August and that central heating in homes is rare.

Men Wear the Pants Here

Women should remember that they're in a male-dominated world. Skirts and dresses are the norm, though this is changing slowly. And "power dressing" — dressing like the foreign stereotypes South Africans have seen on television or in the movies — won't gain you any points at the negotiating table.

The dress code here is more formal and Western than in other African countries. While you can get away with a casual shirtsleeve-no-tie look in a city like Nairobi in Kenya, it won't fly here. Think Europe rather than Africa when it comes to style. Scarves are very popular accessories for women. When dining out or in someone's home, men should wear a jacket and tie to be on the safe side. Sneakers, except in the gym or on the tennis court, are a no-no. If you need casual shoes, invest in a pair of *veldt schoone* (Hush Puppy-like soft safari boots). Everybody wears them.

Mink and Manure

Among wealthy whites in the so-called Mink and Manure Belt of Johannesburg's northern suburbs, grand displays of jewelry, furs and imported *haute couture* were once the rage. But an increase in violent crime has mostly put an end to such ostentation. Still, in certain select shopping malls, you'll find bored, wealthy housewives "dressed to the nines" while food shopping or being coiffed at the hairdresser. ("Big hair" is still a status symbol.)

Sport

South Africans take their golf seriously. If invited to play, leave the loud checks and pastels (Americans, in particular, are very found of these on the links) at home. Take a cue from the man who was South Africa's greatest golfer of all time, Gary Player. Player always dressed in black on the pro golf tour. Nothing flashy about that. Visitors will be surprised at how well dressed the local duffers are. Even the caddies are better dressed than many golfers back in the States. At the more upscale country clubs, dressing in whites is still preferred on tennis and squash courts.

Ethnic Clothing

With the exception of the KwaZulu/Natal region and the Indian areas of major cities, don't expect to see much in the way of traditional ethnic dress on the streets. The Zulus remain the most attached to their traditional attire — a leopard skin with a buffalo headdress decorated with the feathers of a bishop bird or ostrich, an oxhide shield, and oxtail knee ornaments — though these are mostly reserved for formal political occasions, funerals and weddings.

However, traditional print dresses and head scarves have made a comeback for women and are definitely accepted at formal occasions, thanks, in large part, to Winnie Mandela (the estranged wife of President Nelson Mandela), who served to popularize and legitimize the look. Its elegant simplicity is both fetching and practical.

Reading South Africans

Silence: Not Necessarily Golden

Because South Africans are generally bubbly and talkative, silence says a lot. They're polite as well, and if you are boring them, they'll suffer through in silence (unlike the Americans they otherwise admire). When the questions stop, consider it time to go. You've lost your audience.

Hand Gestures

The amount of hand movements a South African uses while talking is a good indicator of the degree of passion that individual has for a particular topic or proposal. However, it's impolite and seen as a personal challenge to point at someone with your index finger wagging. It's also considered rude to talk with your hands in your pockets. The "V" or "peace sign," formed with the middle and index fingers with the palm facing inward, is the equivalent of "giving someone the finger" in the West, and it's usually punctuated by an upward thrust of the hand.

Facial Expressions & Physical Contact

Facial expressions are a highly developed form of communication here. At a business meeting, South Africans will steal glances at one another or at the boss to judge a reaction. Because so much business is done on trust, eye contact is essential, especially in the white community. However, black South African businessmen are more attuned to physical contact. A warm handshake followed by an arm around the shoulder means you've a successful meeting.

"It is much easier to tell how things went after meeting with African businessmen. They're always polite, more so than whites, but they're also more physically demonstrative in their approval," says one British businessman who's been in South Africa for over a decade.

"After one particularly good meeting, my South African counterpart walked me out to my car in the parking lot and for ten minutes never once took his arm off my shoulder. I knew then that we had a deal."

19 Entertaining

Grazing

South Africans are lavish entertainers. Restaurants range from the classically elegant (serving first-rate continental cuisine) to the hearty steak house (great value but lacks atmosphere) to the small Indian specialty cafes (which lack physical appeal but offer the best curries this side of Bombay). If you're the host, be aware that tipping is discretionary, not required.

Most South Africans like to entertain at home, and you'll probably witness something of a Jekyl-and-Hyde transformation in the personality of your South African counterparts as they move from conservative-and-uptight-businessman mode to relaxed, playful, and probably rather drunken hosts on their own turf. Invitations are often issued casually, as in "Why don't you drop by next Tuesday for a *graze*?" (*Graze*, a term befitting a country heavily involved in agriculture and cattle farming, is slang for a meal.) Though such an offer may sound offhand, it's sincere. Check a day or two beforehand to confirm a time.

Business dinners are usually *sans* wives. This is especially true in the black business community, where a female's role isn't a public one.

The Braai

South Africans are true carnivores. Any sufficiently large animal seems to be fair game for consumption in one form or another, from ostrich (low in cholesterol, high in protein), hippo, giraffe, venison, goat, crocodile and warthog (similar to wild boar) to more traditional meats such as lamb and beef. Shellfish is also popular. Vegetarians are simply mocked.

If you spend any length of time here, expect to be invited to a *braai vleis* (literally, cooked meat), the local equivalent of a backyard barbecue or cookout. South Africans consider this social ritual one of the country's greatest contributions to world culture. The cuisine is predictable — steaks, chops and *boerewors* (a local, usually highly spiced sausage not unlike *kilbasa*) washed down with wine and beer. These can be all-day affairs, especially if the home has a swimming pool. (On a per-capita basis, Johannesburg rivals Southern California for home swimming pools. In fact, the Creepy Crawly, the automated pool vacuum and cleaner, was invented here.)

The *braai* amounts to a role reversal for South African males, most of whom would have a difficult time boiling water. But here, the man of the house is in charge of the cooking, and it's common practice for his male friends and colleagues to stand around the grill, inhaling smoke, talking about sports and quaffing beer. Don't expect to order your steak to taste; everything tends to come off the grill in the same well-done, overcooked state. The "girls" will sit in their own little segregated circle discussing babies, servants, or which country would be the best to emigrate to.

The Dinner Party

A step up from the *braai* is the dinner party. These can be fairly formal affairs, with men in coats and ties. Most invitations provide a half-hour "window"; if it reads 7:30 P.M., it's not considered rude to show up at 8. Drinks are always served first, and sometimes the pre-dinner sessions can last as long as the dinner itself. You may be served beef, mutton, curries, pumpkin, rice, green vegetables and other dishes. South Africans like to linger over their meals, and they appreciate both good humor and serious conversation. House servants will cook, serve at table, and clear away and wash the dishes.

Basic Dinner Party Etiquette

- Men should rise when being introduced to other guests for the first time; women should offer their hand to be shaken.
- Never arrive empty-handed. Lavish gifts aren't expected, but flowers, chocolates, or a middle-range-to-expensive bottle of wine will be appreciated.
- Be courteous but not overly friendly to house servants. Don't, for example, engage them in conversation, or both they and the host will feel uncomfortable.
- Continental style (fork in left hand, knife in right) is observed by most. *Serviettes* are napkins.
- Never point or gesticulate with your silverware while engaged in mealtime conversation.
- Salad is served *after* the main course.
- Leaving food uneaten is considered a poor reflection on the host.
- Dessert (possibly fresh fruit) is followed by the cheese course. Coffee is usually taken in a sepa-

rate room with an after-dinner drink. One local specialty is Van Der Hum, a tangerine-based liqueur from the Cape region.

- Smoking is permitted just about everywhere and anytime in South Africa, but when dining in someone's home, wait until the meal is finished.

Adventurous Palates

Consider each meal a culinary safari. Much of South African food tastes better than it looks. In the course of your meals, you'll probably encounter:

Prawns. Mozambican prawns are world famous. Their meat is especially sweet, and they're usually prepared highly spiced (*peri-peri*). Prawns are definitely finger food; just rip the heads off and enjoy. One of the oddest sights you'll see is a group of well-dressed South Africans sitting around a restaurant table, sucking prawn heads.

Snoek (pronounced snuk). This is a white fish found off the Cape peninsula. It's often dried and salted — almost the South African equivalent of a sardine, only bigger.

Bredie. This is basically a mutton stew with a tomato, pumpkin, quince or cabbage base.

Waterblommetjie bredie. Made from water hyacinths that grow in the dams and marshes of the Western Cape region, this is a quasi-mythic dish that everyone talks about but no one seems to eat. One veteran journalist who spent more than a decade in South Africa says he never met a South African who had ever even tasted *waterblommetjie bredie*.

Pap or *Mieliepap*. Boiled corn meal, usually encountered at *braais*. This is true comfort food and is roughly equivalent to grits (a regional specialty of the American South) or Italian polenta. It's also served as a porridge with curdled milk.

Biltong. This is dried salted meat, not unlike jerky. Beef and venison are the most popular, but *biltong* is also commonly made from ostrich, wildebeest or antelope. South Africans living or visiting overseas have been know to go into "*biltong* withdrawal."

Babotie. Of Malay origin, this dish is basically hamburger seasoned with curry and topped with a runny egg (or sometimes dried fruit). It's probably only a matter of time before McDonalds offers a *McBabotie* meal.

Umngqusho. This is basically a corn mush made from dried kernels, beans, sugar, onions potatoes, chilis and lemon and simmered over an open fire. *Umngqusho* has become exceedingly popular in some circles since President Mandela (supposedly) said that it's his favorite food.

Mashonzha **(a.k.a.** *Mopani* **worms).** This is one of those exotic snack foods whose primary purpose seems to be to horrify foreigners. You'll find cans of these crunchy fried caterpillars (usually packed in tomato or chili sauce) in many corner groceries. They're best served with peanuts.

Maheu (pronounced ma-he-oo). This traditional sorghum "beer," thick and sour, is an acquired taste. *Mampoer* and *witblitz* (white lightning) are potent but illegal home brews, similar to schnapps.

Socializing

The Two (or Three or Four) Martini Lunch

The social lunch in South Africa tends to be a boozy affair. Wine is as common at meals as it is in France. (South Africans are extremely proud of their local vintages.) While visitors will not offend by refusing to imbibe, they should expect to be cajoled and jokingly insulted. If invited to "have a few beers with the lads" or "go for a *dop*," accept, even if you have to nurse one of the fine local brews. (Lion Lager is the top seller, probably because of its great advertising tag line: *Down a Lion, Feel Satisfied*. Castle is also popular.) South Africans are loathe to admit it, but deep inside they don't entirely trust someone who is totally abstemious.

South African bars can be smoke-filled and rather loud affairs, places where men are supposed to be MEN. It's only been in the past few years that women have even been permitted to enter. While public drunkenness is common, drunk driving carries harsh penalties.

The Shebeen

In some ways, *shebeens* are symbolic of the defiant attitude of the black majority during the 1950s and 1960s, when alcohol was forbidden to blacks. Home brewing became popular and hundreds of these traditional African drinking houses (complete with loud music, live entertainment and very inexpensive local dishes) sprang up in the townships, attracting an eclectic mix of black professionals and laborers.

Shebeen queens, the female owners of these establishments, became a social class unto themselves, enjoying relative wealth and community respect for their defiance of apartheid laws. It wasn't until 1984 that the white government, tired of the endless police raids that failed to close any *shebeens* for more than a few days at a time, granted the first liquor licenses to 27 Soweto *shebeen* operators.

Today, *shebeens* have moved into the previously all-white suburbs, where they're hot entertainment spots. They tend to draw a racially mixed and younger crowd (unlike many of the country's upper-crust restaurants, which still cater predominately to whites). One of the best is Mama's Jazz Joint in the Johannesburg suburb of Rosebank.

Night Life? Not Really

Nightlife of South Africa's major cities is sparse. Attendance at live theater performances, especially in Johannesburg, has declined in recent years, mainly because of white fears of violent crime. However, South Africans seem obsessed with cinema (both as entertainment and as a source of information about other cultures), perhaps because of tightly controlled TV programming and decades of international isolation. Movie houses (a.k.a. *bioscopes* or cinemas) tend to be crowded, especially on weekend evenings. Foreigners should expect to be quizzed about how closely the life portrayed in a current hot movie corresponds to the reality in their homelands.

Outside of the black townships, there was never much of a nightclub tradition, though in the 1970s, large, racially mixed discotheques proliferated in Johannesburg in defiance of the laws. Virtually all have shut now. Beware the late-night clubs in Durban and Cape Town. They're usually located near the dock areas and cater to a rough clientele.

The Game Parks

South Africans are proud of their country's wildlife, which is on view in Kruger National Park as well as in several private reserves. Kruger boasts more than 450 species of birds and more than 100 species of mammals. To show no interest in this aspect of the country's heritage borders on an insult. South Africa is home to nearly 90 percent of the world's white rhinos (until recently, dangerously close to extinction, due to their popularity as hunting trophies and because their horns are highly valued in Chinese medicine and as dagger handles in Yemen), and African elephants (depleted elsewhere on the continent by poachers) thrive at Kruger to the point where herds are culled each year.

Other local fauna include lions, cheetahs, black rhinos, springboks, blue wildebeest, kudu, elands, warthogs, giraffes, blesboks, buffalo and the rare Cape Hunting Dog.

21   Basic Phrases

English	Afrikaans
Good morning	*Goeie more*
Good-bye	*Tot siens*
How are you / things	*Oe lyk dit?*
Yes	*Ja*
No	*Nee*
I don't understand	*Ek wird nie (slang)*
	Ek verstaan nie (formal)
OK / fine	*goed*
Company / firm	*Maatskappy*
Money	*Kleingeld*
Airport	*Lughawe*
Thank you	*Dankie*
Where do you come from?	*Van waaraf kom jy?*
What's your name?	*Wat is jou naam?*

English	Zulu
Good morning	*Sawubona*
Yes	*Yebo*
No	*Hayi*
Thank you	*Ngiyabonga*
Good-bye	*Hamba kahle*
My name is ____	*Igama lam ngu* ____
What's your name?	*Ubani igama lakho?*

English	Xhosa
Good morning	*Molo*
Yes	*Ewe*
No	*Hayi*
Thank you	*Enkosi*
Good-bye	*Hamba kakuhle*
My name is ____	*Igama lam ngu* ____
What's your name?	*Ungubani igama lakho?*

22 Correspondence

The order of information in a South African address is the same as in the West, and English is the preferred language to use. Virtually every business address will include a post office box number or a "Private Bag" (a large p. o. box) number. Using the street address is optional. Only in the cases of small towns or villages should you use the province name, which follows the mandatory four- digit city or town code. An example:

Office of the Commissioner for Inland Revenue
Frans du Toit Building
303 Paul Kruger Street
P. O. Box 426
Pretoria 0001 (Optional: Gauteng)
Republic of South Africa

When using a document delivery service such as Federal Express or DHL, give the full building and street address, not the p.o. box.

European-style dates are used in correspondence, with the day preceding the month and the year.

23 Useful Telephone Numbers

These are local numbers. If calling from outside South Africa, dial your country's international access code, then South Africa's country code [27], then the city code, omitting the zero (which is only used for in-country calls).

City codes

Johannesburg	011
Cape Town	021
Pretoria	012
Durban	031

Police emergency 0111
Ambulance (national emergency number): . . 10177
Hospitals

Johannesburg	488-4911
Cape Town, Groote Schuur Hospital	404-4141

Taxis (must be phoned for pickup):

Johannesburg	725-3333 or 725-1111
Cape Town	434-4444

Avis car rental (toll free). 08000-21111
Budget car rental (toll free) 08000-16622
Johannesburg International Airport. 975-9963
South African Airways (Johannesburg). . . 333-6504
Rail reservations: (Blue Train). 774-4469/70